The Maui Chef
Seafood Cookbook

Executive Chef Michael Gallagher

ISLAND HERITAGE™
PUBLISHING

ISLAND HERITAGE™
P U B L I S H I N G
A DIVISION OF THE MADDEN CORPORATION

94-411 KŌʻAKI STREET, WAIPAHU, HAWAIʻI 96797

Orders: (800) 468-2800 · Information: (808) 564-8800

Fax: (808) 564-8877

islandheritage.com

ISBN: 1-59700-319-0

First Edition, First Printing, 2006

Photography by David Watersun
Food styled by Dean Louie

DESIGN BY KATHLEEN NAGATA SATO

DEDICATION / ACKNOWLEDGMENTS

- To all the Mauians who dedicate their lives to pursuing their dreams in paradise.

- To the fishermen who battle the elements to bring me the freshest, most beautiful seafood I have ever seen.

- To Thomas, owner of the award-winning Surfing Goat Dairy in Kula, whose goat cheeses rival those of the world.

- To Michael and Melissa McCoy, owners of Fresh Island Herbs in Kula, who have introduced me to microherbs and countless other fruits and vegetables (Have you ever seen a watermelon radish? I hadn't till I met Michael). Mahalo for AAA, your patience and teachings, and for letting me enjoy one of the most natural tropical gardens in the world for five days.

- To Darrel and Angel at Maui Seafood for the freshest fish on the island, big mahalo. It was raining and cold upcountry as we shot our second day of seafood and there was Angel, an hour's drive up the mountain, in the cold rain with the flu. You truly are an angel.

- To David Gridley, owner of Maui Oma Coffee Roasting and president of the Maui Coffee Roasters Association—without his excellent blends, I couldn't have stayed up many a night to write this book.

- To Michael and Darlene Kilinski, who have inspired me to create my own company, MauiChef.com LLC, and who introduced me to Island Heritage and The Madden Corporation.

- Last but certainly not least to Dale Madden, who had the faith in me to bring me into the world of cookbook writing with our first project—the beautifully published and highly acclaimed *Gourmet Cuisine Island Style*, which is truly a work of art. Thank you all for your advice and encouragement, but most of all for your dedication to your expertise.

Lahaina Harbor

TABLE OF CONTENTS

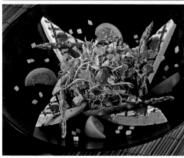

🐟 Entrées

INTRODUCTION

Aloha! Welcome to a taste of Maui. My name is Michael Gallagher, executive chef of the award-winning Sea House Restaurant on beautiful Nāpili Bay at the Nāpili Kai Beach Resort on the island of Maui.

For over fifteen years I have been creating and serving award-winning cuisine on Maui. The natural resources of this beautiful tropical island paradise in the middle of the Pacific Ocean are bountiful and seemingly endless. I have had the enviable opportunity to work with local fishermen and farmers, and to experience the highest quality seafood and produce the islands have to offer—from the tropical rain forests and valleys of Hāna to the nutrient-rich volcanic soil of Haleakalā, with microclimates ideal for a wide array of fruits and vegetables as well as fragrant fresh herbs. The pineapple fields of West Maui produce some of the sweetest hybrid pineapples on the market and on occasion, excellent coffee and sweet white corn. The macadamia nut and honey farms of the north shore are also becoming well known for their quality and varieties. But most of all it is the deep pristine Pacific Ocean that surrounds Maui and offers the healthiest, freshest seafood I have ever seen that is truly my inspiration. What toys for a chef to play with!

From sunrise to sunset and into the night the brave fishermen of Maui go out into the vast ocean to bring in prized *'ahi* (yellowfin tuna), beautiful *mahimahi* (dorado or dolphinfish), the torpedo-like fighting *ono* (wahoo), deepwater *hāpu'upu'u* (sea bass), and the prize of the Pacific: the light, flaky, and moist family of snappers. *'Ōpakapaka* (pink snapper), vibrant *onaga* (red snapper), and *uku* (gray snapper) are among the favorites of chefs, and of customers who come to Maui to dine on our latest preparations of these rare gifts. While fishermen battle the strong winds, storms, and fabled high seas of Hawai'i during the winter months, they keep the supply abundant; they are truly my heroes. I feel I owe it to them to not waste their courageous efforts.

In *The Maui Chef Seafood Cookbook* you will find many time-tested recipes that I have either created or adapted from the island's locals, which you can re-create at home for your friends and family—what we call our *'ohana*. I have provided suitable substitutions whenever possible for ingredients that may be hard to obtain in your local markets. And I have included Web sites from which you can order Hawai'i-specific ingredients to truly give a taste of Maui to your creations.

Happy cooking!

Executive Chef Michael Gallagher

APPETIZERS

Appetizers are the key to impressing friends and family. They should be colorful and flavorful, small yet satisfying. I spend countless hours every week in my kitchen creating and trying new and exciting starters. I have compiled in this book a taste of some of my favorites. I know you will enjoy seeing the smiles on your guests' faces as much as you enjoy making these little dishes. And this is only the beginning!

Farm-Raised Abalone with Hāmākua Mushrooms and Liliko'i Hollandaise

LILIKO'I HOLLANDAISE

2 egg yolks

1 tsp. fresh lemon juice

2 Tbsp. orange-*liliko'i*** juice concentrate** (Hawaiian Sun brand, if available; or orange juice concentrate)

¼ c. clarified butter

Salt and pepper to taste

Place egg yolks, lemon juice, and concentrate in a food processor and blend until smooth, about 30 seconds ✸ Heat butter to 140 degrees ✸ Slowly add butter to sauce, stirring until thick ✸ Add salt and pepper ✸ Serve immediately.

1 Tbsp. canola oil

1 tsp. minced fresh shallots

¼ c. finely julienned Hāmākua mushrooms

1 farm-raised abalone, cleaned, tenderized with a mallet, and finely julienned (reserve shell)

⅛ c. white wine

Salt and pepper to taste

1 serving steamed white rice

3 asparagus stalks, steamed

Heat canola oil in a sauté pan over medium heat ✸ Add shallots, mushrooms, and abalone; sauté 1 minute or until mushrooms are soft and shallots and abalone are lightly browned ✸ Deglaze pan with white wine until wine begins to reduce, about 10 to 15 seconds ✸ Season with salt and pepper, and remove from heat.

Place a ramekin of steamed white rice at top of a heated dinner plate ✸ Put abalone shell on top of rice, and pour deglazed sauce into shell along with sautéed abalone ✸ Lay asparagus alongside rice ✸ Ladle *Liliko'i* Hollandaise over abalone and asparagus ✸ Garnish with finely diced fresh tomato, microgreens, and chopped fresh parsley.

Serves 1.

Although fresh abalone is difficult to find, it is well worth the effort. This recipe was featured on the cover of Maui Menu magazine and has received rave reviews from our guests. I have added Hāmākua mushrooms for their texture and flavor; if unavailable, use any fresh oyster mushroom.

Taro-Crusted Crisp Pacific Portabella Soft-Shell Crab Roll with Red Curry–Coconut Butter Sauce

SUSHI RICE

1 c. cooked sticky rice, room temperature	1 tsp. rice vinegar	1 tsp. sugar

Toss all ingredients in a small bowl.

RED CURRY–COCONUT BUTTER SAUCE

1 tsp. red curry paste (available in Asian markets)	1/4 c. coconut syrup	1/4 lb. unsalted butter
	1/4 c. heavy whipping cream	Salt and pepper to taste

Place curry paste and coconut syrup in a small saucepan; bring to a boil over high heat ❧ Whisk until smooth, then add cream ❧ Bring to a boil, then lower heat to a simmer; cook until sauce is reduced by half ❧ Slowly whisk in butter ❧ Remove from heat and strain through a fine sieve ❧ Add salt and pepper.

1/4 c. olive oil	Canola oil for frying	8 oz. taro chips
1/8 tsp. salt	1 soft-shell crab, cleaned and head removed	1 c. panko flakes (Japanese bread crumbs)
1/8 tsp. coarsely ground black pepper	1 c. tempura batter (prepare according to package directions)	1 sheet dried nori seaweed (available in Asian markets)
1 portabella mushroom, cleaned		1 c. Sushi Rice

Preheat grill ❧ Mix olive oil, salt, and pepper in a shallow bowl; coat mushroom with mixture ❧ Grill mushroom until soft, about 2 minutes on each side (or bake until soft) ❧ Let mushroom cool, then thinly slice and set aside ❧ Preheat frying oil to 350 degrees ❧ Dip crab in tempura batter, then fry until golden brown, 3 to 4 minutes ❧ Remove crab from oil and place on paper towels to absorb excess oil ❧ Place taro chips and panko flakes in a food processor and blend for 30 seconds, until coarsely chopped ❧ On a clean cutting board, lay nori sheet ❧ Spread rice over seaweed, leaving 1/2 inch at top of sheet ❧ Place crab and mushroom in center of rice ❧ Using a bamboo sushi roller or your hands, roll tightly. (Wet end of seaweed with a little water to help it stick together) ❧ Dip roll in tempura batter, then roll in taro crust ❧ Deep-fry until golden brown, about 3 minutes ❧ Remove roll and place on paper towels to absorb excess oil.

Using a very sharp chef's knife, cut sushi roll ends off, then cut roll on a bias at center ❧ Ladle Red Curry–Coconut Butter Sauce in center of a dinner plate and place sushi halves standing upright in center ❧ Garnish with Thai chile oil, sesame seeds, and finely julienned green onions.

Serves 1.

Coconut and Macadamia Nut–Crusted Tiger Prawns with Sweet Thai Chile–Maui Honey Sauce

SWEET THAI CHILE–MAUI HONEY SAUCE

¼ c. sweet Thai chile sauce
(Mae Ploy brand, if available)

¼ c. Maui honey

¼ c. rice vinegar

1 tsp. minced fresh ginger or roasted garlic (optional)

¼ c. canola oil

Place all ingredients except oil in a blender; blend until smooth ❧ Keep blending while slowly adding oil, until thickened.

Canola oil for frying

1 c. panko flakes
(Japanese bread crumbs)

¼ c. macadamia nuts, toasted

¼ c. coconut flakes

8–12 tiger prawns, peeled, deveined, and butterflied

1 c. flour seasoned to taste with salt and freshly ground black pepper

1 c. tempura batter
(prepare according to package directions; if unavailable, use whipped fresh eggs, but crust may not be as crisp)

Preheat frying oil to 350 degrees ❧ Blend panko flakes and macadamia nuts in a food processor for 20 seconds; mix in coconut flakes ❧ Lightly dust each prawn in seasoned flour, then tempura batter, and finally in panko crust ❧ Deep-fry prawns in oil for about 3 minutes or until golden brown ❧ Remove from oil and place on paper towels to absorb excess oil.

Ladle ¼ cup of Sweet Thai Chile–Maui Honey Sauce onto center of a plate ❧ Place 2 prawns on top of sauce ❧ Garnish with finely diced Maui pineapple and chopped green onions.

Serves 4.

Everyone loves fried shrimp, and this recipe will keep them coming back for more. If you can't wait to get an order of Maui honey, you can substitute your favorite honey in this recipe.

Maui Fish-and-Chip Trio

SPICY SOY MIRIN

½ c. soy sauce

½ c. mirin
(sweet Japanese rice wine)

1 tsp. minced fresh ginger

½ tsp. crushed red chile pepper

½ tsp. white sesame seeds

Place all ingredients in a small saucepot and bring to a boil ❧ Reduce heat and simmer 5 minutes ❧ Chill until ready to serve.

Canola oil for frying

1 egg, beaten

2 c. flour

1 c. cold water

1 Tbsp. curry powder (optional)

Salt and pepper to taste

4 2-oz. slices (½ lb.) fresh *mahi* fillet

4 2-oz. slices (½ lb.) fresh *ono* fillet

4 2-oz. slices (½ lb.) fresh *hāpu'upu'u* (sea bass) fillet

1 Hawaiian sweet potato, thinly sliced into chips and deep-fried

Preheat frying oil to 350 degrees in a thick-bottom soup pot or home fryer.

In a mixing bowl, place egg and 1 cup of flour ❧ Whisk in cold water just until smooth, being careful not to overmix. (Whisk in curry powder for additional flavor and color) ❧ Place remaining flour in a separate bowl; season with salt and pepper ❧ Lightly coat fish in flour, then in egg batter ❧ Fry until golden brown and fish is cooked through, 3 to 4 minutes ❧ Place on paper towels to absorb excess oil.

Fill a small bowl or ramekin with ¼ cup Spicy Soy Mirin, and place in center of a warm plate ❧ Arrange 1 piece of each fish around sauce ❧ Place chips in between fish, and garnish with chopped fresh herbs such as cilantro or chervil.

Serves 4.

Hamachi Sashimi

LEMON OIL

½ c. canola oil

2 Tbsp. fresh lemon zest

1 Tbsp. sugar

1 tsp. crushed red chile pepper

1 Tbsp. minced fresh
lemongrass bulb (optional)

Place all ingredients in a small saucepot ❧ Warm slowly until sugar has dissolved, being careful
not to heat oil over a near simmer ❧ Remove from heat when lemon zest begins to bubble ❧ Let
cool for 1 hour ❧ Cover and refrigerate overnight ❧ Strain through a fine sieve and refrigerate
until needed.

8 shiso (Japanese basil) leaves
(or lemon or cinnamon basil)

1 c. Wasabi-Shoyu Vinaigrette
(see Maui Napoléon Poke
Trio Salad)

½ lb. skinless, boneless fresh
hamachi, blood line removed

1 tsp. Hawaiian sea salt
(or your favorite sea salt)

Chill 4 sushi-style plates (I prefer black rectangular plates) ❧ Place 2 shiso leaves in center of
each plate, with leaves pointing in opposite directions ❧ Fill ramekins with ¼ cup of Wasabi-
Shoyu Vinaigrette; place 1 in center of each plate ❧ Using your sharpest knife, slice hamachi
paper thin, cutting against the grain for tenderness as you would with any meat ❧ Place equal
amounts of sashimi on each side of ramekins ❧ Lightly drizzle Lemon Oil over sashimi ❧ Very
lightly sprinkle a pinch of sea salt over fish on each plate ❧ Garnish with fresh lemon wedges.

Serves 4.

Hamachi, *the
Japanese name
for young
yellowtail, is
prized in Japan,
California,
Hawai'i, and in
sushi bars all
over the world.
This sweet and
firm yet succulent
fish has a rich,
buttery flavor
and is best eaten
sushi style. I have
also added an
interesting
dipping sauce to
spark the palate.
You will need a
very sharp sushi
knife, or if you
are lucky you
may be able to
buy the hamachi
presliced paper
thin.*

*A guest once asked
me, "Michael, how
come you do not
have crab cakes
on the menu?" I
explained that
every restaurant
has crab cakes and
that I wanted to be
different. No sooner
had the words left
my mouth that I
realized the truth
of the age-old
proverb, "The cus-
tomer is always
right!" So I set out
to make a crab cake
I could be proud of.
I've combined snow
crab with tiger
prawns and sea
scallops, and incor-
porated Hawaiian
chile peppers and
pineapple into the
sauce and relish. An
option for enhanced
flavor and presenta-
tion is the addition
of mango purée
with a squirt bottle.*

Maui Avocado Crab Cakes with Hawaiian Chile Pepper–Ginger Aïoli

HAWAIIAN CHILE PEPPER–GINGER AÏOLI

¼ c. Hawaiian chile pepper jelly
(available through Island Plantations' line of gourmet jams, jellies, and syrups)

1 tsp. minced fresh ginger

Juice 1 fresh lime

¾ c. mayonnaise

Salt and pepper to taste

Place all ingredients except salt and pepper in a food processor; blend until smooth, about 1 minute ❧ Season with salt and pepper ❧ Using a funnel, pour aïoli into a squirt bottle for easier presentation.

MAUI PINEAPPLE–CHILE RELISH

1 c. ¼-in. diced Maui pineapple

¼ c. ¼-in. diced Maui onion
(or Vidalia or Wala Wala onion)

2 Tbsp. Thai chile sauce
(available at Asian markets)

1 Tbsp. finely sliced fresh cilantro

Toss all ingredients in a medium bowl ❧ Cover and chill until ready to serve.

4 tiger prawns, peeled and deveined

4 sea scallops

½ Maui onion
(or Vidalia or Wala Wala onion), **diced**

¼ c. mayonnaise

1 tsp. sambal oelek
(Indonesian chile paste; if unavailable, use chile paste)

1 lb. snow crabmeat, excess water squeezed out

1 avocado, peeled, seeded, and ½-in. diced

1 c. panko flakes
(Japanese bread crumbs)

Salt and pepper to taste

1 c. flour

4 eggs, whipped

Canola oil for frying

Place prawns, scallops, onion, mayonnaise, and chile paste into a food processor; blend until smooth, about 30 seconds ❧ Scrape mixture into a medium bowl; add crab, avocado, ½ cup panko flakes, salt, and pepper, and mix gently with hands until combined ❧ Portion seafood mix into 8 individual cakes of equal size ❧ Coat each cake with flour, then egg, then panko. (Optional: blend macadamia nuts with remaining panko flakes in food processor before breading cakes) ❧ Deep-fry cakes in oil preheated to 350 degrees, or pan-fry, until golden brown, 5 to 7 minutes ❧ Remove from heat and place on paper towels to absorb excess oil.

On a warm dinner plate, zigzag Hawaiian Chile Pepper–Ginger Aïoli back and forth across plate. (Optional: turn plate a quarter turn and zigzag mango purée across aïoli) ❧ Cut 2 crab cakes in half and arrange around center of plate in a circle ❧ Place a tablespoon of Maui Pineapple–Chile Relish on center of crab cakes ❧ Garnish with microgreens and toasted sesame seeds.

Serves 4.

Seared Onaga with Guava-Ginger Vinaigrette and Candied Macadamia Nuts

GUAVA-GINGER VINAIGRETTE

1/2 c. guava juice concentrate

1 tsp. minced fresh ginger

1/2 small Maui onion
(or Vidalia or Wala Wala onion), chopped

2 Tbsp. rice vinegar

1 tsp. chopped fresh cilantro

3/4 c. canola oil

Salt and pepper to taste

Combine guava concentrate, ginger, onion, vinegar, and cilantro in a blender; blend until smooth ❧ Keep blending while slowly adding oil, to desired consistency ❧ Season with salt and pepper.

CANDIED MACADAMIA NUTS

1/4 c. water

1/4 c. sugar

1/2 c. chopped macadamia nuts, toasted

Preheat oven to 325 degrees ❧ In a small bowl, whip water and sugar together until sugar has dissolved ❧ Toss nuts in sugar water and spread on a Teflon cookie sheet (or a regular pan sprayed with nonstick spray) ❧ Roast in oven for 15 minutes or until nuts begin to brown and liquid has dried up ❧ Remove from heat and let cool at room temperature; remove from pan ❧ Break up brittle into smaller pieces if necessary.

2 Tbsp. canola oil

1 lb. skinless, boneless fresh *onaga* fillet
(or your favorite local snapper)

1/4 c. flour seasoned to taste with salt and freshly ground black pepper

4 plum tomatoes, sliced

Heat canola oil in a sauté or frying pan over high heat ❧ Lightly dust *onaga* fillets in seasoned flour; sear fillets in oil, lightly browning on both sides ❧ Remove from heat and place on paper towels to absorb excess oil. (Note: Because I use only the freshest fish, right out of ocean, I serve this medium rare to preserve the natural textures and flavors of the fish. Should there be a question about the freshness of your fish, finish cooking it in an oven preheated to 400 degrees.)

Place 3 slices of plum tomato in center of a warmed dinner plate ❧ Place 1 piece of *onaga* on top of tomatoes ❧ Ladle 1/4 cup of Guava-Ginger Vinaigrette over *onaga*, and sprinkle Candied Macadamia Nuts around plate ❧ Garnish with freshly chopped parsley, toasted sesame seeds, and an edible flower.

Serves 4.

Onaga, or red snapper, has long been one of my favorite fish. I used to have it flown up from Florida when I was executive chef at the Yankee Clipper Restaurant in Sea Girt, New Jersey, and it has always been a crowd favorite. The Pacific onaga has an even more delicate flavor than the Atlantic snapper and is very moist and flaky. I have always enjoyed pan-searing it. With this vinaigrette and candied macadamia nuts, you will truly enjoy a taste of paradise.

I love Italian food and I love tiger prawns, so it was only natural that I would come up with this recipe eventually. Easy to prepare yet loaded with flavors and textures, this recipe is one of my favorites. The secret is to use very good Italian bread—I use roasted garlic, black pepper, and Asiago pugliese bread.

There are some very good pestos on the market but there is none better than fresh pesto. I have substituted macadamia nuts for pine nuts for a Hawaiian twist.

Pesto Prawn Bruschetta with Grilled Kula Vine-Ripened Tomato Coulis

10 fresh basil leaves	1/8 c. shredded Asiago cheese	1/4 tsp. salt
1/4 c. chopped fresh curly-leaf parsley	1/8 c. macadamia nuts (or pine nuts), **toasted**	1/4 c. olive oil
1/4 c. chopped fresh baby spinach	1/2 tsp. coarsely ground black pepper	8 tiger prawns, 8–12 size, peeled and deveined

Place all ingredients except oil and prawns into a food processor ✦ Blend for 30 seconds ✦ Keep blending while slowly adding oil, about another 30 seconds ✦ Place in a small bowl ✦ Thinly slice tiger prawns and stir them into pesto ✦ Cover and refrigerate.

GRILLED KULA VINE-RIPENED TOMATO COULIS

1 Maui onion (or Vidalia or Wala Wala onion), **cut in half**	4 Kamuela vine-ripened tomatoes (or your favorite vine tomato), **cut in halves**	1 tsp. balsamic vinegar
		1 tsp. fresh tarragon
	2 Tbsp. olive oil	1 tsp. sugar (optional)

Preheat grill ✦ Rub onion and tomatoes with oil ✦ Grill until soft, 4 to 6 minutes; remove from grill and let cool ✦ Place onion and tomatoes in a food processor with balsamic and tarragon; blend until smooth, about 1 minute ✦ Strain through a fine sieve into a saucepan ✦ Bring coulis to a boil, then reduce heat and simmer for 5 minutes ✦ If tomatoes are too tart, add sugar.

2 Tbsp. butter, softened	4 slices Italian bread

Preheat oven to 350 degrees ✦ Butter bread and place slices on a sheet pan ✦ Spread prawn pesto over bread and bake until lightly brown, 8 to 10 minutes.

Place equal amounts of Grilled Kula Vine-Ripened Tomato Coulis in center of 4 warm dinner plates ✦ Place bread on top of coulis ✦ Garnish with a drizzle of balsamic vinegar, finely diced fresh tomato, chopped fresh parsley, and shredded Asiago cheese.

Serves 4.

This combination of the famous Kula goat cheese and renowned Kona crab is a delectable start to any gourmet meal. If you have ever rolled a soft taco or burrito it is the same concept, just smaller and tighter.

Kula Goat Cheese and Kona Crab Lumpia

Canola oil for frying

½ c. finely julienned Maui onion
(or Vidalia or Wala Wala onion)

½ c. finely julienned won boc
(or napa cabbage)

1 small carrot, finely julienned

8 oz. Kona crabmeat
(or dungeness or your favorite lump crabmeat)

½ c. Kula goat cheese

4 large fresh sweet basil leaves, finely julienned

Salt and freshly ground black pepper to taste

8 lumpia wrappers
(or won ton wrappers)

4 servings spring lettuce greens

Kapis manis (or sweet shoyu) **for drizzling**

Fill a small pan with water and bring to a boil; lightly blanch (submerge in boiling water for 30 seconds) onion, cabbage, and carrot ❧ Pour vegetables into a strainer in the sink and run cold water over them; set aside ❧ In a small bowl, combine crabmeat and goat cheese using a rubber spatula ❧ Season mixture with basil, salt, and pepper. (Mixture can be covered and chilled until ready to prepare.)

Lay 1 lumpia wrapper on a clean cutting board, with 1 corner facing you ❧ Place ⅛ of crab mixture onto lower half of wrapper, then add ⅛ of vegetable mixture just above crab mixture ❧ Roll bottom corner over mixture, then fold side corners over to seal edges ❧ Continue rolling; wet top corner with water and seal roll tightly, with top corner lying on cutting board ❧ Repeat steps to create 8 lumpia in all.

Preheat frying oil to 350 degrees ❧ Place lumpia in oil and fry until golden brown, 3 to 4 minutes ❧ Place on clean paper towels to absorb excess oil.

Place lumpia on cutting board and cut off very ends of wrapper, then cut in half on a bias ❧ Place 4 halves of lumpia on a plate next to your favorite spring mix of lettuce greens ❧ Drizzle soy sauce over lettuce greens ❧ Garnish plate with fresh microgreens or sprouts and chopped macadamia nuts.

Serves 4.

Dynamite Rainbow Sushi Pizza with Sweet Soy Sauce

DYNAMITE AÏOLI

¾ c. mayonnaise

2 tsp. sambal oelek
(Indonesian chile paste; if unavailable, use chile paste)

1 tsp. wasabi
(Japanese green horseradish) **paste**

1 Tbsp. chopped fresh cilantro

2 Tbsp. finely chopped green onions

Juice 1 lime

Salt and pepper to taste

Place all ingredients in a food processor and blend until smooth, about 30 seconds.

---

4 cooked pizza shells, 4–6 in. in diameter

1 c. Dynamite Aïoli

1 c. finely julienned romaine lettuce
(or your favorite lettuce)

½ lb. 'ahi, thinly sliced

½ lb. hamachi

1 avocado, peeled, seeded, and sliced into 12 wedges

Shoyu (sweet soy sauce) **for drizzling**

¼ c. red tobiko caviar

¼ c. green wasabi tobiko caviar
(both caviars available through Eskimo Candy, or frozen at seafood markets)

Preheat oven to 400 degrees and warm pizza shells ❧ Fill a small ramekin with Dynamite Aïoli, reserving remainder of aïoli, and refrigerate until ready to serve ❧ Remove pizza shells from oven and spoon equal amounts of aïoli onto each shell ❧ Place equal amounts lettuce in center of shell ❧ Place 1 slice 'ahi on lettuce, then overlap with 1 slice hamachi, then 1 slice avocado; repeat steps 3 more times around pizza shell ❧ Drizzle sweet soy sauce over each pizza, then make small football shapes around shell with the 2 caviars (alternate, using 2 teaspoons) ❧ Garnish with a sprinkling of toasted sesame seeds and microgreens.

Cut pizza into quarters and place in a circle on a warm dinner plate, with points of slices facing outward ❧ Place ramekin of Dynamite Aïoli in center of plate for dipping.

Serves 4.

I fell in love with sushi when I came to Maui. With the abundance of fresh fish it was only a matter of time until I was to create my own version of my newfound passion. This is a combination of many of my favorites—'ahi (yellowfin tuna), hamachi (yellowtail), avocado, and of course Dynamite Aïoli, which I must say is only for the bravest of spice lovers.

Baked Stuffed Sea Scallops with Maui Mango Butter

MAUI MANGO BUTTER

2 tsp. canola oil

2 Tbsp. minced Maui onion
(or Vidalia or Wala Wala onion)

1 fresh mango, peeled, seeded, and finely diced

1/8 c. mirin
(sweet Japanese rice wine)

1/2 lb. butter

In a small saucepan, heat canola oil over medium heat; sauté onions until lightly brown ❧ Add mango and mirin; simmer for 10 minutes or until reduced by half ❧ Slowly whisk in butter ❧ Remove from heat and strain with a fine sieve.

1 c. snow crabmeat

2 Tbsp. mayonnaise

1 tsp. dry mustard
(Coleman's brand, if available)

2 Tbsp. chopped green onion

Salt and pepper to taste

12 sea scallops in the shell

1 c. baby spinach

2 c. rock salt

1 tsp. blue food coloring
(optional)

Preheat oven to 375 degrees ❧ In a small bowl, mix crab, mayonnaise, mustard, and green onion ❧ Season with salt and pepper, and refrigerate until ready to serve ❧ Stuff each scallop with equal amount of stuffing ❧ Place scallops on a sheet pan and bake for 15 minutes or until lightly brown.

Lightly blanch (submerge in boiling water) or steam spinach ❧ Pour through a strainer, then into a bowl of ice water, to keep spinach bright green; drain ❧ Season with salt and pepper; set aside ❧ In a medium bowl, mix rock salt with food coloring.

Place equal amount of rock salt into 4 large soup bowls ❧ Place 3 scallops in each bowl ❧ Place equal amount of spinach on top of each scallop ❧ Spoon Maui Mango Butter over each scallop ❧ Garnish with finely diced tomato and microgreens.

Serves 4.

I love the presentation of this dish as well as its flavors. A little blue food coloring and rock salt give the illusion that these scallops are still in their Pacific surroundings (you will need large white soup bowls for the full effect). Although fresh is always best, sea scallops are hard to find, and in the shell even harder; you can instead use the IQF (Individually Quick Frozen) sea scallops in the shell, available at any wholesale seafood purveyor or ordered through your local fish market buyer.

SOUPS AND SALADS

We all love a good soup. As a child, you probably remember your parents stirring up a pot of soup when you were under the weather—as much for comfort as for health. In this day and age, health advice often comes in the form of fresh salads. Here, I've taken salad creation to new heights, with an emphasis on Hawai'i's best seafood and fresh local ingredients.

Fresh Island Herbs farm

Sea House Chowder

3 Tbsp. butter

1 Maui onion
(or Vidalia or Wala Wala
onion), 1/4-in. diced

1 Tbsp. minced fresh garlic

3/4 c. chopped celery

3 Tbsp. flour

3 c. canned clam juice

2 c. heavy cream

1 c. peeled, diced Idaho potato

1 tsp. salt

1/4 tsp. black pepper

2 tsp. chopped fresh thyme or
1 tsp. dried thyme

1 c. canned chopped
sea clams

1 c. diced skinless
fresh *ono* fillet
(or *mahimahi* or your
favorite white fish)

Melt butter in a large thick-bottom stockpot over medium heat ❧ Add onions, garlic, and celery and stir until lightly brown ❧ Add flour and cook until flour and butter are incorporated, about 2 minutes ❧ Slowly whisk in clam juice and bring to a boil, then reduce to simmer and cook for 1/2 hour ❧ Slowly whisk in cream ❧ Add potatoes, seasonings, clams, and fish and simmer over low heat for 10 minutes more, or until potatoes are soft ❧ Pour soup into 6 soup bowls.

Serves 6.

I created this recipe to give my guests and employees at the Sea House Restaurant a taste of Back East. (To get really close to home, add chopped apple-wood–smoked bacon just before the onions and brown.) Ono was the perfect choice as its meaty flavor and steak-like texture hold up well in a chow-der, plus we get the freshest ono I have ever tasted!

Kona Crab Chowder

1 large or 2 small ears fresh corn, shucked

¼ lb. unsalted butter

1 c. ¼-in. diced Maui (or Vidalia) onions

1 c. ¼ c.-in. diced celery

1 Tbsp. minced fresh garlic

¼ c. flour

3 c. crab stock (made from fresh crab shells; if unavailable, use clam juice)

1 c. heavy whipping cream

2 Idaho potatoes, cleaned, peeled, and ½-in. diced

1 Tbsp. chopped fresh basil

1 Tbsp. chopped fresh oregano

1 Tbsp. chopped fresh thyme

1 bay leaf

1 lb. Kona crabmeat

Preheat grill ❧ Grill corn, and let cool; cut kernels off and reserve ❧ Melt butter in a large thick-bottom stockpot over medium heat ❧ Add onions, celery, and garlic, and stir until lightly brown ❧ Add flour and cook until flour is incorporated, about 2 minutes ❧ Slowly whisk in stock and bring to a boil; reduce heat and simmer for ½ hour ❧ Slowly whisk in cream and continue simmering ❧ Add potatoes, herbs, crab, and corn and simmer over low heat for another 10 minutes, or until potatoes are soft.

Pour soup into 4 soup bowls and garnish with thinly sliced green onions.

Serves 4.

Uku and Tiger Prawn Bisque
with Tobiko Crème Fraîche

2 bay leaves

1 Tbsp. whole black peppercorns

1 tsp. pickling spices

1 small Maui onion
(or Vidalia or Wala Wala
onion)**, chopped**

2 celery stalks, chopped

2 carrots, chopped

2 cloves fresh garlic

1 c. dry sherry

**1 c. puréed fresh vine-
ripened tomato**

1 qt. shrimp stock
(made from fresh shrimp shells;
if unavailable, use shrimp base
and 1 qt. water)

1 c. flour

1 c. melted butter

1 qt. heavy whipping cream

12 tiger prawns
(16–20 size)**, peeled, deveined,
and chopped**

**1 lb. skinless, boneless fresh
uku fillet** (or your favorite snapper
or sea bass)**, diced**

Salt and pepper to taste

1 ¹/₂ c. crème fraîche

1 tsp. tobiko caviar

Tie bay leaves, peppercorns, and pickling spices in cheesecloth ❧ Sauté onion, celery, and carrots in a medium stockpot until golden brown ❧ Add garlic, sherry, and tomato, and simmer for 15 minutes ❧ Add shrimp stock and spices in cheesecloth, and simmer for 1 hour ❧ Make a roux by combining flour and butter ❧ Slowly whip roux into stock until smooth; simmer for 10 minutes ❧ Slowly whip in cream, then add prawns and *uku* and simmer 5 more minutes, until prawns are cooked through ❧ Season with salt and pepper, and keep warm over low heat until ready to serve ❧ In a small bowl, combine crème fraîche and tobiko caviar; stir with a spoon until blended.

Place ³/₄ cup of bisque into each large soup bowl ❧ Spoon 1 tablespoon of Tobiko Crème Fraîche in center of bisque ❧ Garnish with fresh parsley or chervil.

Serves 12.

Back in 2000, I was invited to Taste of Hawai'i on the island of Kaua'i to cook for charitable causes. I created this recipe for the event using farm-raised Kaua'i tiger prawns. Over 500 servings later, it was a success! Since then I have added uku (gray snapper) and switched to Indonesian tiger prawns, as the Kaua'i farm unfortunately closed down. Every time I taste this soup I will always remember my trip to that beautiful island.

I remember my first night dive on Maui for spiny lobsters almost 15 years ago. What an exciting adventure! Hawaiian lobsters are a delicacy, and this recipe highlights their true richness. The secret is in the stock. Although making stock will take some time, it is well worth the effort and can be refrigerated up to a week, or frozen in small batches for up to 3 months.

Cream of Maui Lobster Soup

MAUI LOBSTER STOCK

2 Tbsp. canola oil

1 Maui onion
(or Vidalia or Wala Wala onion)**, chopped**

¼ c. dry sherry

2 c. chopped celery

2 c. chopped carrots

4 bay leaves

1 Tbsp. pickling spices

2 Tbsp. whole black peppercorns

1 c. tomato paste

2 gal. cold water

2 Tbsp. Hawaiian sea salt
(or your favorite sea salt)

2 whole Maui spiny lobsters
(or Maine lobsters)

Heat oil in a large stockpot over high heat ❧ Add vegetables and stir until lightly brown ❧ Add spices and tomato paste; stir until incorporated, about 1 minute ❧ Add water and sea salt and bring to a boil ❧ Carefully add lobsters to water and boil, covered, for 4 minutes ❧ Carefully remove lobsters from stock and reduce heat to a simmer ❧ Rinse lobsters under cold water to cool ❧ Remove claw and tail meat; dice and reserve ❧ Place all shells and bodies back into stock, and simmer for 2 hours ❧ Strain stock through a fine sieve.

3 Tbsp. butter

1 Maui onion (or Vidalia or Wala Wala onion)**,
¼-in. diced**

1 Tbsp. minced fresh garlic

¼ c. dry sherry

3 Tbsp. flour

3 c. Maui Lobster Stock
(or best lobster base available mixed with 3 c. warm water)

2 c. heavy cream

Melt butter in a large thick-bottom stockpot over medium heat ❧ Add onions and garlic, and stir until lightly brown ❧ Add sherry and bring to a boil ❧ Add flour and cook until flour and butter are incorporated, about 2 minutes ❧ Slowly whisk in lobster stock and bring to a boil, then reduce to simmer and cook for ½ hour ❧ Slowly whisk in cream and simmer 10 minutes more ❧ Add reserved lobster meat and remove pot from heat.

Serves 6.

Hawaiian Lobster, Prawn, and Avocado Salad

ORIENTAL AÏOLI

³/₄ c. mayonnaise

¹/₄ c. soy sauce

1 tsp. rice vinegar

1 Tbsp. mirin
(sweet Japanese rice wine)

1 Tbsp. minced pickled ginger

¹/₂ tsp. sesame oil

Combine all ingredients in a mixing bowl ❧ Chill until ready to serve.

1 c. chopped cooked Hawaiian lobster

1 c. chopped cooked Hawaiian prawns

1 c. Oriental Aïoli

2 ripe avocados, cut in half, seed and skin removed

4 c. chopped fresh romaine lettuce

Combine seafood with ¹/₂ cup Oriental aïoli and mix until well coated ❧ Place equal amounts of seafood mixture into avocado halves ❧ Place an avocado in center of a chilled large salad plate or soup bowl ❧ Place lettuce around avocado ❧ Drizzle remaining aïoli over greens. Garnish with grape or cherry tomatoes, cucumber slices, julienned carrots, fresh microgreens, and fried julienned won ton skins or fried Asian noodles.

Serves 4.

I recently created this special salad for my guests at the Sea House Restaurant and sold it out every night! You can substitute Maine lobster and shrimp if you cannot find the Hawaiian species. This simple recipe is a seafood lover's dream.

Maui Asparagus and Organic Tofu Salad with Cantonese Vinaigrette

CANTONESE VINAIGRETTE

1 tsp. minced fresh ginger	1 Tbsp. rice vinegar	1 tsp. sugar
1/8 c. hoisin sauce (available in Asian markets)	1/2 tsp. sambal oelek (Indonesian chile paste; if unavailable, use chile paste)	2 Tbsp. canola oil 1/8 tsp. salt

Combine all ingredients in a blender and blend until smooth, about 20 seconds.

10 fresh asparagus stalks, cleaned	1/2 lb. organic hard tofu, cut into 6 triangles	1/2 head romaine lettuce (or your favorite lettuce), roughly chopped

Preheat grill ❧ Blanch (submerge in boiling water) asparagus and cut each piece into thirds; set aside ❧ Grill tofu triangles until light brown ❧ Let cool.

Place lettuce in center of a chilled triangle plate or your favorite salad plate ❧ Place tofu around lettuce and asparagus around tofu, then drizzle Cantonese Vinaigrette over all ❧ Garnish with toasted sesame seeds, chopped green onions, finely julienned carrots, and microgreens.

Serves 2.

SOUPS AND SALADS

Maui asparagus is a specialty item; if unavailable, find the freshest asparagus you can in your local market. For the tofu, I use an organic hard tofu—it is easier to cut, grill, and work with than the silken tofu. This dish is very popular with my vegetarian friends as well as my health-conscious guests.

I created this
recipe for Maui
Chefs Presents
2005, a local
charity event
where 12 top
Maui chefs
cook together
at the Hyatt
Regency in
Kā'anapali
for a night in
the first week
of September.
If you get the
chance, it is
an event not
to miss!

Gallagher's Island Poisson Cru

AVOCADO–VINE TOMATO SALSA

1 ripe avocado, peeled, seeded, and finely diced

1 vine-ripened tomato, finely diced

1/2 small Maui onion (or Vidalia or Wala Wala onion)**, finely diced**

1/4 c. seeded and finely diced fresh cucumber

1 Tbsp. fresh lemon juice

1/2 tsp. sambal oelek (Indonesian chile paste; if unavailable, use chile paste)

1 tsp. chopped fresh basil

1/4 tsp. Hawaiian sea salt (or your favorite sea salt)

1/4 tsp. coarsely ground black pepper

Place all ingredients into a medium bowl and carefully stir with a wooden spoon ❧ Cover and refrigerate until ready to serve.

COCONUT CURRY VINAIGRETTE

1/4 c. coconut syrup

1 tsp. red curry paste (available in Asian markets)

1 tsp. minced fresh ginger

1 tsp. chopped fresh cilantro

2 Tbsp. rice vinegar

1/4 c. canola oil

Place all ingredients except oil in a blender and blend until smooth, about 30 seconds ❧ Keep blending while slowly adding oil.

2 Tbsp. chopped fresh cilantro

2 Tbsp. chopped fresh basil

1/2 tsp. coarsely ground black pepper

1/2 lb. skinless, boneless fresh *ono* center cut, cut into a block

2 Tbsp. canola oil

1/4 c. fresh coconut milk (or frozen coconut milk)

1/4 c. fresh lime juice

12 baby spinach leaves

4 won ton skins, cut into circles and deep-fried

Mix herbs and pepper in a shallow bowl ❧ Dredge *ono* block in herbs to coat all sides ❧ Heat canola oil in a sauté pan over high heat; sear all sides of *ono* block, about 10 seconds on each side ❧ Remove from pan and let cool ❧ Place coconut milk, lime juice, and leftover herbs in a blender; blend until mixed, about 20 seconds ❧ Place marinade into a small bowl ❧ Thinly slice seared *ono* block and place slices into marinade; cover and refrigerate 8 to 10 hours. (The acid from the lime juice will finish cooking the fish ceviche style.)

Place 1 tablespoon of Avocado–Vine Tomato Salsa in center of a chilled salad plate ❧ Place 2 slices of *ono* on top of salsa, then 2 leaves of spinach on top of fish, then a won ton chip on top of spinach ❧ Repeat these steps again ❧ Top second chip with 2 leaves of spinach, then 2 slices of fish, then another tablespoon of salsa ❧ Place Coconut Curry Vinaigrette in a squirt bottle and drizzle back and forth over the poisson cru tower ❧ Garnish top with microgreens and sprinkle toasted sesame seeds around plate.

Serves 2.

I have found goat cheese to be an acquired taste—you either love it or hate it. There are many types of goat cheese, each with a distinct flavor and texture. Surfing Goat Dairy has won many awards for their creative, high-quality goat cheese made fresh here on the volcanic slopes of Haleakalā. I prefer the chèvre style of goat cheese. If you cannot obtain the Maui cheese, chèvre is sold in most supermarkets.

Kula Goat Cheese, Maui Papaya, and Baby Spinach Salad with Citrus Vinaigrette

CITRUS VINAIGRETTE

1 tsp. fresh lime juice

1 tsp. fresh lemon juice

2 Tbsp. orange-*liliko'i* juice concentrate (Hawaiian Sun brand, if available; or orange juice concentrate)

2 Tbsp. Maui honey

1 tsp. minced fresh ginger

2 Tbsp. canola oil

Salt and pepper to taste

Place all ingredients in a blender and blend until smooth, about 20 seconds.

1 c. fresh baby spinach

1 ripe Maui papaya, peeled, seeded, quartered, and thinly sliced into fans

¼ lb. Kula chèvre goat cheese, shaped into 6 balls (using a small scooper) **or into 6 quenelles** (using a teaspoon)

Place spinach in a small bowl and toss with Citrus Vinaigrette ❧ Place salad in center of a chilled salad plate ❧ Arrange 3 papaya fans around spinach, then 3 goat cheese balls in between the papaya ❧ Garnish salad with chopped toasted macadamia nuts, then finely julienned carrot, and finally fried Maui onions.

Serves 2.

Fresh Herb–Crusted 'Ahi
with Wasabi-Shoyu Vinaigrette

WASABI-SHOYU VINAIGRETTE

1 tsp. wasabi (Japanese green horseradish) **paste**

2 Tbsp. shoyu
(sweet soy sauce; Aloha low sodium brand, if available)

1 tsp. rice vinegar

1/2 tsp. minced fresh ginger

1 tsp. minced Maui onion
(or Vidalia or Wala Wala onion)

1 tsp. mirin
(sweet Japanese rice wine)

2 Tbsp. canola oil

Place all ingredients in a blender and blend until smooth, about 20 seconds.

1 Tbsp. chopped fresh basil

1 Tbsp. chopped fresh cilantro

1 Tbsp. chopped fresh curly-leaf parsley

1/2 tsp. salt

1/2 tsp. coarsely ground black pepper

1/2 lb. fresh 'ahi, cut into 2 blocks

1 Tbsp. canola oil

1/2 c. salad greens

Place all herbs and seasonings in a shallow bowl and mix well ❧ Roll 'ahi blocks in herb mixture to coat ❧ Heat oil in a sauté pan over high heat; sear 'ahi blocks, 5 to 10 seconds on each side ❧ Remove from heat; let cool for 2 minutes ❧ With a very sharp knife, slice blocks into slices as thin as possible.

Place salad greens in center of a chilled salad plate ❧ Arrange 'ahi slices around greens ❧ Drizzle Wasabi-Shoyu Vinaigrette over all ❧ Garnish greens with fresh kogane sprouts and pickled ginger.

Serves 2.

Tuna, fresh herbs, and an unusual blend of Asian and Hawaiian flavors come together in this recipe to create a healthy, light, and refreshing salad. I love using fresh 'ahi (yellowfin tuna) when available; big-eye tuna is just as good. For a garnish, I use fresh kogane sprouts from Fresh Island Herbs in Kula. Kogane is in the cabbage family and is very prevalent in Japanese cuisine. I love the sprouts, which tend to be sweeter than the peppery radish sprouts.

Tako-Shiitake Kim Chee

1 head won boc (napa) cabbage, finely julienned

1 cucumber, seeded and finely sliced

1 c. shiitake mushroom caps, finely julienned

2 Tbsp. sea salt

1/4 c. rice vinegar

2 Tbsp. sambal oelek (Indonesian chile paste; if unavailable, use chile paste)

1/2 lb. cooked Hawaiian tako (or sushi-grade octopus; available in seafood markets), thinly sliced

Place cabbage, cucumber, and mushrooms in a large bowl and toss well with sea salt; let stand for 1 hour ❧ Squeeze all excess water out of mixture ❧ In another bowl, whisk together vinegar and chile paste ❧ Soak tako in vinegar mixture ❧ Combine tako mixture with vegetable mixture; cover and refrigerate for at least 6 hours.

Serve kim chee alone on a chilled salad plate, or alongside grilled fish and steamed rice.

Serves 2.

Tako is what we call octopus in Hawai'i. Many locals free dive for it (it takes what is called the "tako eye" to spot it). I was introduced to kim chee while working at the Maui Marriott over 10 years ago. Since then I have added many different ingredients to create this salad for spicy kim chee lovers all over the world.

Maui Onion and Kona-Raised Maine Lobster Salad with Balsamic Glaze

2 small Maui onions
(or Vidalia or Wala Wala onions), **peeled**

2 Tbsp. unsalted butter

¼ c. balsamic glaze
(Roland brand, if available)

1 Tbsp. canola oil

1 tsp. minced fresh garlic

1 vine-ripened tomato,
finely diced

1 Tbsp. chopped fresh basil

1 Tbsp. finely diced prosciutto

¼ lb. Kona lobster meat
(or your favorite lobster meat), **finely diced**

1 c. salad greens

Preheat oven to 400 degrees ❧ Cut each onion horizontally to 1 inch from bottom, then vertically, so onions appear quartered but are still intact ❧ Place onions on a sheet pan ❧ Place half of butter in center of each onion, then drizzle 1 teaspoon balsamic glaze over each ❧ Bake until soft, about 10 minutes ❧ Heat canola oil in a large frying pan over high heat ❧ Sauté garlic, tomato, basil, and prosciutto until warm ❧ Add lobster and toss until hot, about 3 minutes.

Place salad greens in center of a salad plate ❧ Place onion on top of greens ❧ Pour lobster mixture over onion and greens ❧ Drizzle remaining balsamic glaze back and forth over entire plate ❧ Garnish with microgreens and sunflower sprouts.

Serves 2.

Maui Napoléon Poke Trio Salad

'AHI POKE

2 oz. 'ahi, finely diced

¹⁄₈ tsp. sea salt

2 Tbsp. fresh seaweed, chopped
(available in Asian markets)

Mix all ingredients in a small bowl ❧ Chill.

CUCUMBER-MANGO NAMASU

¹⁄₂ tsp. sugar

1 tsp. rice vinegar

¹⁄₄ c. very thinly sliced cucumber, seeded

1 Tbsp. finely diced fresh mango

1 Tbsp. finely julienned Maui onion
(or Vidalia or Wala Wala onion)

1 tsp. finely julienned fresh carrot

Whisk sugar and vinegar together in a small bowl ❧ Add rest of ingredients to bowl and toss ❧ Chill.

LOMI SALMON

1 Tbsp. finely diced salted salmon

2 Tbsp. finely diced vine-ripened tomato

1 tsp. thinly sliced green onion

1 tsp. finely diced Maui onion
(or Vidalia or Wala Wala onion)

Combine all ingredients in a small bowl ❧ Chill.

WASABI-SHOYU VINAIGRETTE

1 tsp. wasabi (Japanese green horseradish) **paste**

2 Tbsp. shoyu
(sweet soy sauce)

1 tsp. rice vinegar

2 Tbsp. canola oil

Whisk all ingredients together in a small bowl ❧ Chill.

Place a circle mold in center of a chilled dinner plate ❧ Arrange greens around mold ❧ Place 'Ahi Poke into mold first, then Cucumber-Mango Namasu, and finally Lomi Salmon; press down firmly ❧ Carefully remove mold, using a spoon to hold down contents ❧ Drizzle Wasabi-Shoyu Vinaigrette over all ❧ Garnish with seaweed salad and tobiko caviar.

Serves 1.

This recipe is all about the Pacific Rim! This combination of some of my favorite salads is fresh, healthy, flavorful, and colorful. I bought a special stainless-steel ring mold just for this recipe, which you can find in various sizes at most restaurant supply stores. They are well worth the few dollars they will cost to create some beautiful presentations.

Smoked Marlin Salad with Creamy Horseradish–Fresh Herb Vinaigrette

CREAMY HORSERADISH–FRESH HERB VINAIGRETTE

1 Tbsp. prepared horseradish	2 fresh sweet basil leaves	1 Tbsp. white wine vinegar
1 Tbsp. chopped green onion	1 tsp. chopped fresh tarragon	¼ c. canola oil
1 Tbsp. chopped curly-leaf parsley	1 Tbsp. fresh lemon juice	Salt and pepper to taste
	¼ c. crème fraîche (or sour cream)	

Combine all ingredients in a blender and blend until smooth, about 25 seconds.

½ c. salad greens	¼ lb. smoked marlin, thinly sliced	6 grape tomatoes (or cherry tomatoes)

Place salad greens in center of a chilled salad plate ❧ Arrange marlin around greens ❧ Pour Creamy Horseradish–Fresh Herb Vinaigrette into a squirt bottle and drizzle back and forth over all ❧ Place tomatoes around the marlin ❧ Garnish with finely sliced Maui onions, capers, and fresh microgreens or sprouts.

Serves 2.

Photo by Romeo Collado

ENTRÉES

The main course can either make or break an evening. I have found that fresh ingredients and simple preparations are the key to success. My entrées aim to honor the brave fishermen who bring their delicious catches into my kitchen. I hope your guests are as pleased as mine to enjoy the results.

Macadamia Nut–Crusted Ono
with Lobster-Saffron Beurre Blanc

LOBSTER-SAFFRON BEURRE BLANC

1 tsp. canola oil

1 tsp. minced fresh shallots

1/4 c. dry sherry

1/4 c. heavy whipping cream

1/4 c. fresh lobster stock
(or best lobster base available mixed with 1/4 c. warm water)

1/4 lb. unsalted butter

1/2 tsp. saffron threads

2 Tbsp. finely diced steamed fresh Maine lobster meat

Salt and pepper to taste

Heat canola oil in a medium saucepan ✤ Add shallots and lightly brown ✤ Deglaze pan with sherry and reduce by half ✤ Add cream and lobster stock and bring to a boil; reduce heat and simmer until cream mixture has reduced by half, about 15 minutes ✤ Slowly whisk in butter until incorporated ✤ Add saffron threads and lobster meat ✤ Season with salt and pepper and keep warm until ready to serve.

1/2 c. panko flakes
(Japanese bread crumbs)

1/4 c. chopped macadamia nuts

2 7-oz. skinless, boneless fresh *ono* steaks

1/2 c. flour seasoned with salt and pepper

3 eggs, beaten

1/4 c. canola oil

2 servings steamed rice

Preheat oven to 400 degrees ✤ Place panko flakes and macadamia nuts in a food processor and blend until mixed, about 15 seconds ✤ Dredge *ono* steaks in flour, then in eggs, then in the macadamia nut crust.

Heat a sauté pan over medium heat and add canola oil ✤ Lightly brown both sides of steaks ✤ Place steaks on a sheet pan in the oven ✤ Depending on thickness of fillets, cooking time will vary from 8 to 12 minutes. (Use a knife to look inside fillets to see if more cooking time is needed.) I prefer to serve this fish medium to medium rare.

Fill a timbale mold or ramekin with your favorite steamed rice (I use Indian Harvest Jasmine Blend) ✤ Place in center of a warm dinner plate ✤ Ladle 1/3 cup of Lobster-Saffron Beurre Blanc around rice ✤ Place fish on top of rice ✤ Serve with steamed fresh vegetables, such as French green beans, baby carrots, edamame beans, and yellow wax beans ✤ Garnish with seaweed salad (or finely julienned green onion), tobiko caviar, and chopped fresh curly-leaf parsley.

Serves 2.

Ono (also known as wahoo) is a white fish highly prized in the islands. Since it is firm like steak, people assume it should be grilled. However, this cooking method tends to dry out the fillets. My macadamia nut crust and pan-searing method helps keep moisture in the fish. I then came up with this butter sauce to enhance its flavor and because I love lobster with saffron—they were made for each other!

Crisp Purple Sweet Potato–Crusted Lehi with Pohā Berry Dipping Sauce

POHĀ BERRY DIPPING SAUCE

You can make this simple recipe in minutes. All you need is a food processor.

1 8-oz. jar pohā jam (available through Island Plantations)

¼ c. sushi vinegar (or rice vinegar)

¼ c. canola oil

Blend all ingredients until smooth.

Oil for frying

2 purple sweet potatoes (or your favorite sweet potato)

1 c. panko flakes (Japanese bread crumbs)

4 6-oz. skinless, boneless fresh *lehi* fillets (or your favorite snapper)

½ c. flour seasoned with salt and pepper

2 eggs, beaten

¼ c. canola oil

4 servings steamed white or jasmine rice

Preheat frying oil to 350 degrees ❧ Thinly slice sweet potato into chips and soak in cold water for at least 15 minutes ❧ Rinse chips well and pat dry with a paper towel ❧ Deep-fry until golden brown ❧ Let cool. (Optional: To save time, you can substitute packaged sweet potato chips) ❧ Preheat oven to 350 degrees ❧ In a food processor, roughly chop chips with panko flakes about 30 seconds.

Lightly coat each fillet with seasoned flour, then dip in egg, then coat in sweet potato crust ❧ In a frying pan over medium heat, pan-fry both sides of fillets in canola oil ❧ Finish baking in oven until fish is golden brown and cooked through, 3 to 5 minutes.

Place steamed rice in center of a warm dinner plate ❧ Lay fish on rice and to the side of rice ❧ Drizzle some sauce over fish and rice; serve rest of sauce in a small bowl for dipping ❧ Garnish with fresh pohā berries, if available, or your favorite greens.

Serves 4.

Banana-Crusted Ehu with Hawaiian Vanilla Bean–Coconut Butter Sauce

HAWAIIAN VANILLA BEAN–COCONUT BUTTER SAUCE

2 Hawaiian vanilla beans
(or Tahitian vanilla
beans), **split**

¼ c. coconut syrup (available
through Island Plantations)

1 tsp. minced fresh ginger

½ c. heavy whipping cream

1 lb. unsalted butter

Salt and pepper to taste

Place beans, syrup, ginger, and cream in a thick-bottom saucepan and bring to a boi ❖ Reduce heat to a simmer and reduce sauce by half, about 15 minutes ❖ Slowly whip in butter until dissolved ❖ Remove from heat and season with salt and pepper ❖ Let stand for 15 minutes, then strain through a fine sieve and keep warm until ready to serve.

1 c. panko flakes (Japanese bread
crumbs)

2 Tbsp. chopped fresh parsley

1 c. dried banana chips

**4 6-oz. skinless, boneless fresh
ehu fillets** (or your favorite
snapper or sea bass)

**½ c. flour seasoned with salt
and pepper**

2 eggs, beaten

¼ c. canola oil

4 servings steamed rice

Preheat oven to 350 degrees ❖ Blend panko flakes, parsley, and banana chips in a food processor until roughly chopped, about 30 seconds.

Lightly coat each fillet with seasoned flour, then dip in egg, then coat in banana crust ❖ In a frying pan over medium heat, pan-fry both sides of fillets in canola oil ❖ Finish baking in oven until fish is golden brown and cooked through, 3 to 5 minutes.

Place steamed rice in center of a warm dinner plate. (I like Indian Harvest's colorful Bamboo Rice, which can be made with sautéed Maui onion for extra flavor.) Ladle ¼ cup of sauce below rice ❖ Place fillet on sauce and garnish with grilled bananas or banana chips.

Serves 4.

Ehu is a red snapper that only grows up to 12 pounds and is found in waters up to 1,000 feet deep. This moist, flaky fish is prized among local fishermen and considered a Hawaiian delicacy. I created this recipe with banana, coconut, and Hawaiian vanilla bean to enhance the delicate flavor of the ehu. Hawai'i is the only state in the nation where we have the appropriate soil, temperature, humidity, and climate to grow vanilla orchids; the Big Island is having great success with this crop. The chefs are in heaven.

Steamed Mahi
with Mango Purée and Spicy Chinese Long Beans

MANGO PURÉE

1 fresh mango, peeled, seeded, and chopped

¼ c. mirin
(sweet Japanese rice wine)

Salt and pepper to taste
(optional)

Place mango and mirin in a blender and blend until smooth, about 30 seconds ❧ Season with salt and pepper ❧ Strain puréed mango through a fine sieve; cover and refrigerate.

½ gal. water

½ lb. fresh ginger

½ lb. lemongrass
(or 3 fresh lemons, cut in halves)

2 7-oz. skinless, boneless fresh *mahimahi* fillets

1 lb. Chinese long beans
(or your favorite green beans), cleaned, ends cut, and halved

¼ c. sweet Thai chile sauce
(available at Asian markets)

Place water, ginger, and lemongrass into a wok (or bottom of a metal steamer) and bring to a boil; reduce heat and simmer for 15 minutes ❧ Place fillets in a bamboo steamer basket (or metal steamer) over water ❧ Bring heat to high; cover and steam for 10 minutes ❧ Carefully remove top of steamer and place beans on top of fish; cover and steam for another 5 minutes, or until beans are soft and fish is cooked through ❧ Remove from heat ❧ Place vinaigrette in a medium bowl and toss beans until coated.

Place beans in center of a warm dinner plate ❧ Place steamed *mahimahi* on top of beans ❧ Ladle Mango Purée over all ❧ Garnish with finely julienned red bell pepper that has been soaked in ice water for 10 minutes, then drained.

Serves 2.

I wanted to come up with a very healthy dish that had no butter or cream yet was full of natural flavors and textures—an easy task when surrounded by a bountiful selection of nature's best. I use bamboo steamer baskets over a wok in this preparation, but a metal vegetable steamer would be a good substitute. Mahimahi, also known as dorado or dolphinfish (not the same as dolphin), is a moist and delicate fish, yet firm enough to grill if you prefer that to steaming. What I like most about this recipe is that it is colorful and flavorful while still being very healthy.

Almost every sea-food restaurant has a cioppino or a bouillabaisse on its menu. This is my version of the classic, combining the best Maui has to offer—'ōpaka-paka, mahimahi, ono, 'ahi, and hāpu'upu'u—as well as a great sauce! If you cannot find any taro bread, try Portuguese sweet bread; dipping bread in this sauce is a must.

Maui Bouillabaisse of Fresh Island Fish

¹/₄ c. extra virgin olive oil

1 lb. Maui onions
(or Vidalia or Wala Wala onions), 1-in. diced

2 Tbsp. minced fresh garlic

1 lb. vine-ripened Kula tomatoes
(or your favorite vine tomato), 1-in. diced

¹/₄ lb. red bell pepper,
¹/₂-in. diced

¹/₄ lb. celery, ¹/₄-in. diced

¹/₄ c. Pernod

1 c. fish stock
(or clam juice)

2 Tbsp. chopped fresh basil

2 Tbsp. saffron threads

1 tsp. salt

1 tsp. coarsely ground
black pepper

¹/₄ lb. each 'ōpakapaka,
mahimahi, ono, 'ahi, and hāpu'upu'u, all 1-in. diced

4 slices taro bread

2 Tbsp. butter, softened

2 servings your favorite
cooked pasta

Heat olive oil in a large thick-bottom stockpot ❧ Add onion, garlic, and vegetables, and lightly brown, 5 to 7 minutes, stirring frequently ❧ Add Pernod and increase heat to high to burn off alcohol ❧ Add fish stock, basil, saffron, salt, and pepper; bring to a boil, then reduce heat and simmer for 45 minutes ❧ Add all fish and simmer until fish is cooked through, 10 to 12 minutes.

Toast and butter bread ❧ Place cooked pasta in 2 large soup bowls and ladle equal amounts of bouillabaisse into each ❧ Place 2 slices of toasted bread on edge of each bowl ❧ Garnish with finely julienned red bell peppers soaked in olive oil and fresh basil, and a sprig of fresh flat-leaf parsley.

Serves 2.

Lū'au-Style Uku

½ lb. unsalted butter

½ lb. Maui onions
(or Vidalia or Wala Wala onions), ½-in. diced

1 Tbsp. minced fresh ginger

3 lb. taro leaf
(or baby spinach)

1 can frozen coconut milk

¼ c. coconut syrup

3 c. fish stock
(or clam juice) 1 lb. skinless, boneless fresh *uku* fillet, 1-in. diced

1 tsp. sea salt
(optional)

1 tsp. coarsely ground black pepper

2 servings steamed white rice

Melt butter in a large thick-bottom stockpot over medium heat ❧ Add onions and ginger; lightly brown, about 5 minutes ❧ If using taro leaf, add now as it needs to cook for at least an hour to take out its bitterness and what locals call "itchy mouth." Add coconut milk, syrup, and fish stock; bring to a boil, then reduce heat and simmer, covered, for 1 hour ❧ Add fish and simmer until fish is cooked through, 10 to 12 minutes. (If using spinach, add now) ❧ Season with salt and pepper.

Place steamed white rice in center of 2 large soup bowls, then ladle equal amount of fish *lū'au* over rice ❧ Garnish with seaweed salad and tobiko caviar.

Serves 2.

Uku is Hawaiian gray snapper and is firmer than its relatives the 'ōpakapaka and onaga. Smaller uku (under 12 pounds) are best, for as this fish gets larger it becomes tougher. At traditional lū'au, I came across a dish called squid lū'au, which locals love. It is made mainly with coconut milk and lū'au (taro) leaf. I've re-created this dish using its core ingredients and adding some of my favorite. If lū'au leaf is hard to come by, use fresh baby spinach.

Taro-Crusted Hapu
with Miso-Peanut Vinaigrette

MISO-PEANUT VINAIGRETTE

¼ c. golden miso paste
(available in Asian markets and some health food stores)

¼ c. chunky peanut butter

¼ c. rice vinegar

¼ c. mirin
(sweet Japanese rice wine)

¼ c. honey

¼ c. cold water

1 Tbsp. chopped fresh ginger

1 tsp. sambal oelek
(Indonesian chile paste; if unavailable, use chile paste)

1 Tbsp. fresh cilantro

¼ c. canola oil

Combine all ingredients except oil in a blender and blend until smooth, about 45 seconds; if too thick, add a little more water ❧ Keep blending while slowly adding oil ❧ Cover and refrigerate.

½ c. taro chips
(available at www.MauiChef.com and some Pacific specialty stores)

½ c. panko flakes
(Japanese bread crumbs)

2 7-oz. skinless, boneless fresh *hāpu'upu'u* fillets
(or your local sea bass or *mahimahi*)

½ c. flour seasoned with salt and pepper

2 eggs, beaten

¼ c. canola oil

2 servings steamed rice

2 Tbsp. shoyu
(sweet soy sauce)

Preheat oven to 400 degrees ❧ Blend taro chips and panko flakes in a food processor for 15 seconds, until chips are roughly chopped but still visible ❧ Dredge fish in flour, then in egg, then in taro crust ❧ Heat canola oil in a large frying pan over medium heat; lightly brown fish about 2 minutes on each side ❧ Place fish on a sheet pan; bake until fish is just cooked through, 8 to 12 minutes depending on thickness of fillets.

Place a ramekin of steamed rice in center of a warm dinner plate. ❧ Ladle Miso-Peanut Vinaigrette around rice ❧ Place fish on top of rice ❧ Drizzle shoyu back and forth over fish ❧ Place a taro chip in center of fish ❧ Garnish with chopped fresh parsley, and microgreens or sprouts.

Serves 2.

Steamed Moi with Hot Sesame

½ gal. water

½ lb. fresh ginger, roughly chopped

½ lb. lemongrass, roughly chopped
(or 3 fresh lemons, cut in half)

8 6- to 8-oz. fillets boneless fresh *moi*, skin on

4 whole baby bok choy

¼ c. sesame oil

4 servings steamed basmati rice

1 tsp. minced fresh garlic

¼ c. chopped fresh cilantro

Place water, ginger, and lemongrass into a wok or double boiler steamer and bring to a boil, then reduce heat and simmer for 15 minutes ❧ Place *moi* fillets in a bamboo steamer basket or steamer pan and turn heat to high; cover and steam for 5 minutes ❧ Carefully remove top of steamer and place bok choy on top of fish; cover and steam for another 5 minutes or until cabbage is soft and fish is cooked through ❧ Meanwhile, heat sesame oil in a small frying pan over high heat until just beginning to smoke.

Place rice in center of a warm dinner plate ❧ Cut bok choy in half and arrange around rice ❧ Place 2 fillets on top of rice, then place equal amounts of garlic and cilantro on top of each fish ❧ Carefully pour 1 tablespoon of hot sesame oil over garlic and cilantro to sear ❧ Garnish with julienned green onions and sesame seeds.

Serves 4.

Passion Fruit–Marinated Grilled Hebi

1 8-oz. jar passion fruit (*liliko'i*) **jelly** (available through Island Plantations)

1 Tbsp. **sushi vinegar** (or rice vinegar)

1 tsp. **minced fresh ginger**

1 tsp. **crushed red chile pepper**

¼ c. **canola oil**

4 6-oz. skinless, boneless fresh

hebi **steaks (or tuna or marlin)**

1 whole **pineapple**, sliced into 4 round slices and grilled

Blend jelly, vinegar, ginger, and pepper in a blender; slowly add canola oil until thickened, about 30 seconds ✤ Chill half of marinade to use as a dipping sauce ✤ Place other half of marinade in a mixing bowl; add fish and thoroughly coat ✤ Cover and marinate in refrigerator for 2 hours ✤ Preheat grill to medium-high heat ✤ Grill pineapple first, then grill fish until cooked through, about 4 minutes on each side; discard marinade.

Place grilled pineapple on plate. (If you can find ti or banana leaves, they make a great liner for the plate) ✤ Place fish on top of pineapple and drizzle reserved marinade on top of fish ✤ Garnish with fresh fruit salsa or diced pineapple.

Serves 4.

Hebi (also known as short-bill spearfish) has an amber-colored flesh that is softer and more delicate than most other billfish. Hebi has a mild flavor and is great on the grill as an alternative to tuna or marlin.

Onaga Laulau

4 ti leaves

2 skinless, boneless fresh
onaga **fillets**

¹/₄ c. mayonnaise

1 Tbsp. oyster sauce

4 slices Maui onions
(or Vidalia or Wala Wala
onions), **¹/₄-in. thick**

**4 slices vine-ripened
Kula tomatoes**
(or your favorite vine
tomato), **¹/₂-in. thick**

1 tsp. tobiko caviar

¹/₂ c. baby spinach

¹/₂ tsp. sea salt

**¹/₂ tsp. coarsely ground
black pepper**

Overlap 2 ti leaves and place an *onaga* fillet in center of leaves ❧ Mix mayonnaise and oyster sauce together, and spread over fillet ❧ Place 2 slices of onion, then 2 slices of tomato on top of mayonnaise mix ❧ Season with salt and pepper ❧ Top with tobiko caviar and spinach ❧ Wrap ti leaves around fillet and tie with stems of leaves, so that a basket is created for fish to steam in. ❧ Place in a steamer over boiling water, and steam for 15 minutes.

Serve *laulau* on a large dinner plate with steamed white rice and Lomi Salmon (see Maui Napoléon Poke Trio Salad) ❧ Unwrap *laulau* at the table, and the steam and effervescence will impress your guests.

Serves 2.

Laulau is another favorite among islanders. It is usually made with steamed pork, butterfish, and lū'au leaf— all steamed in ti leaves and served with steamed white rice and poi. Since I have never been a big fan of poi or butterfish, I again decided to play around with the ingredients, while keeping the traditional method and presentation. Ti leaves may be hard to come by, so if unavailable, use banana leaves or bake in parchment paper.

Tilapia has been farmed for food for over 2,500 years. Originally a native species of Africa and the Middle East, tilapia is found today in tropical waters around the world. Tilapia was introduced to Hawai'i in the 1950s and soon became abundant and popular for keiki (children's) fishing contests. It has an excellent flavor and is very mild. Did you know that in 1998 astronaut John Glenn took tilapia into space for an aquaculture experiment?

Pan-Fried Tilapia with Hāmākua Oyster Mushrooms and Garlic Butter

¹/₄ c. canola oil

8 5- to 6-oz. skinless, boneless fresh tilapia fillets
(or your favorite white fish)

1 c. flour seasoned with salt and pepper

1 c. julienned Hāmākua oyster mushrooms
(or your favorite mushrooms)

2 Tbsp. minced fresh garlic

¹/₄ c. white wine

Juice 1 fresh lemon

¹/₄ lb. unsalted butter

Salt and pepper to taste

2 Japanese eggplants, grilled and cut into quarters

Heat canola oil in a large skillet or frying pan over medium-high heat ❧ Lightly coat fish in flour and pan-sear in oil for about 3 minutes ❧ Turn over fillets and add mushrooms and garlic ❧ Fry for 2 minutes or until garlic begins to brown ❧ Add wine and lemon; reduce heat to medium and simmer 2 minutes ❧ Turn off heat and remove fish ❧ Add butter to pan and stir until dissolved ❧ Season with salt and pepper.

Place 2 pieces of eggplant in center of a warm dinner plate ❧ Place fish on top of eggplant and pour mushroom garlic butter over fish.

Serves 4.

Cajun-Seared Rainbow Runner with Maui Honey Butter

4 6-oz. skinless, boneless fresh rainbow runner fillets

¼ c. Cajun spice (Chef Paul Prudhomme brand, if available)

¼ c. canola oil

¼ c. white wine

1 8-oz. jar Maui honey (available through Island Plantations)

½ lb. unsalted butter

Heat pan over high heat ❧ Lightly coat fillets in Cajun spice ❧ Add oil to pan and sear fish on 1 side until blackened, 3 to 4 minutes ❧ Turn fish over and add white wine; reduce heat to a simmer ❧ Add honey and butter and simmer until fish is cooked through, 2 to 3 more minutes ❧ Remove fish.

Ladle sauce onto center of a warm dinner plate ❧ Place fillets on sauce ❧ Garnish with diced fresh fruit such as papaya, kiwi, or cantaloupe.

Serves 4.

Rainbow runner (also known as Hawaiian salmon) is not really a salmon but a relative of the kingfish family. The pink, moist fillets are complemented by the spice and sweetness of the sauce in this recipe. A cast-iron pan is best for searing; otherwise, use a nonstick pan.

Grilled 'Ahi Steaks with Wasabi Aïoli, Tobiko Caviar, and Ginger–Kaffir Lime Butter Sauce

WASABI AÏOLI

1/2 c. mayonnaise	1 Tbsp. wasabi (Japanese green horseradish) **paste**	1/8 tsp. salt
	1 Tbsp. fresh lemon juice	1/8 tsp. pepper

Place all ingredients in a blender and blend until smooth, about 20 seconds ❧ Place in a squirt bottle and refrigerate until ready to serve. (Aïoli can be made a day in advance.)

GINGER–KAFFIR LIME BUTTER SAUCE

1 Tbsp. canola oil	2 Tbsp. minced pickled ginger	1/2 c. heavy whipping cream
2 Tbsp. finely diced Maui onion (or Vidalia or Wala Wala onion)	4 fresh kaffir lime leaves (or 1 tsp. lime juice concentrate)	1/4 lb. unsalted butter (Plugrá brand, if available)
	1/4 c. mirin (sweet Japanese rice wine)	Salt and pepper to taste

Heat canola oil in a medium saucepan over medium heat ❧ Add onions and lightly brown ❧ Add ginger, lime leaves, and mirin, and bring to a boil ❧ Add cream; return to a boil, then reduce heat and simmer until cream has thickened, about 15 minutes ❧ Slowly whip in butter until dissolved ❧ Season with salt and pepper.

2 8-oz. 'ahi steaks	1/4 tsp. salt	2 servings steamed white rice
2 Tbsp. canola oil	1/4 tsp. coarsely ground black pepper	

Preheat grill ❧ Brush 'ahi steaks with canola oil, then season with salt and pepper ❧ Grill steaks 1 to 2 minutes on each side, depending on thickness of steaks.

Place a ramekin of steamed white rice in center of a warm dinner plate ❧ Ladle Ginger–Kaffir Lime Butter Sauce around rice ❧ Place 'ahi steak on top of rice ❧ Drizzle Wasabi Aïoli back and forth across steak ❧ To garnish, place sunflower sprouts on top of 'ahi, then tobiko caviar on top of sprouts; sprinkle black sesame seeds around plate.

Serves 2.

This dish is dedicated to Dorothy Millar, one of the founders of the Napili Kai Beach Resort, who recently passed away. She loved pāpio, and I always located some for her every time she came to town. Pāpio is also known as pompano and is light, mild, and flaky (if the fish are small). Pan-seared with flour, salt and pepper, and lemon, this fish can stand on its own with no need for fancy sauces. But since I love sauces, I couldn't help but add a touch of Hawai'i to this dish.

Pan-Seared Pāpio
with Lemon-Caper-Liliko'i Butter Sauce

2 7-oz. skinless, boneless fresh *pāpio* fillets

1/2 c. flour seasoned with salt and pepper

2 Tbsp. canola oil

1 Tbsp. minced fresh shallots

1/4 c. white wine

Juice 1/2 fresh lemon

2 Tbsp. orange-*liliko'i* or passion fruit juice concentrate (Hawaiian Sun brand, if available; or orange juice concentrate plus 1 tsp. sugar)

1/4 c. heavy cream

1/4 lb. butter

1 Tbsp. capers

Salt and pepper to taste

Dredge *pāpio* fillets in seasoned flour ❧ Heat canola oil in a large frying pan over medium heat ❧ Fry fillets until almost cooked through, about 3 minutes on each side, depending on their thickness ❧ Remove fillets and place on paper towels to absorb excess oil ❧ Place shallots in frying pan in remaining oil; lightly brown, about 1 minute ❧ Add wine and lemon juice, and simmer until reduced by half ❧ Add concentrate and cream, and simmer until cream thickens ❧ Slowly whisk in butter until dissolved ❧ Add capers, and season with salt and pepper.

Place fish on a large platter and pour sauce over fillets ❧ Garnish with lemon slices and chopped fresh parsley.

Serves 2.

Ponzu Plum–Glazed Grilled Shutome

PONZU PLUM GLAZE

½ c. canned plum sauce	**¼ c. honey**	**1 tsp. sambal oelek**
¼ c. plum wine	**¼ c. canola oil**	(Indonesian chile paste; if unavailable, use chile paste)
¼ c. ponzu sauce		

Combine all ingredients in a blender and blend until smooth, about 30 seconds.

2 7-oz. skinless, boneless fresh   ¾ c. Ponzu Plum Glaze
center cut *shutome* steaks

Preheat grill ✤ Marinate steaks in ½ cup of glaze for 2 to 4 hours ✤ Remove steaks and discard marinade ✤ Grill steaks for 3 to 4 minutes on each side, depending on thickness of steaks, being careful not to overcook. (While grilling, baste steaks with ¼ cup of glaze.)

Place steaks on a large platter ✤ Garnish with toasted sesame seeds, green onions, pickled ginger, and lemongrass sprigs ✤ Use remaining glaze for a dipping sauce.

Serves 2.

ENTRÉES

Shutome, the Pacific swordfish, is a great grilling fish and very forgiving to the novice cook. Marinating this fish for a few hours before heating up the grill only adds to its superb texture and richness. (All marinade ingredients are available in Asian markets.) The marinade is also used for basting, to prevent the fish from drying out, and as a dipping sauce when dinner is served.

Oven-Roasted Hawaiian Spiny Lobster with Pickled Ginger–Lemon–Sake Butter Sauce

PICKLED GINGER–LEMON–SAKE BUTTER SAUCE

1 Tbsp. canola oil

1 Tbsp. minced pickled ginger

1 Tbsp. minced fresh shallots

¼ c. sake
(Japanese rice wine)

Juice 1 fresh lemon

¼ c. heavy whipping cream

¼ lb. unsalted butter

Salt and pepper to taste

Heat canola oil in a medium saucepan over medium heat ❧ Add ginger and shallots; lightly brown, about 30 seconds ❧ Add sake and lemon juice, and reduce by half ❧ Add cream and reduce until thickened, about 5 minutes ❧ Slowly whisk in butter until dissolved ❧ Remove from heat ❧ Season with salt and pepper.

2 7-oz. Hawaiian spiny
lobster tails, split

4 oz. Pickled Ginger–Lemon–
Sake Butter Sauce

Preheat oven to 350 degrees ❧ Place lobster tails on a sheet pan and ladle ¼ cup of sauce on each tail ❧ Bake until lobster is cooked through, 10 to 12 minutes, depending on thickness of tail.

Place lobster on a large platter with your choice of starch and vegetables ❧ Pour remaining sauce over tails just before serving ❧ Garnish platter with chopped fresh parsley and lemons cut into rounds.

Serves 2.

Asian-Barbecued Opah
with Green Papaya–Maui Mango Salad

ASIAN BARBECUE SAUCE

¹/₂ c. hoisin sauce
(available in Asian markets)

¹/₂ c. canned plum sauce
(available in Asian markets)

1 tsp. peeled, minced fresh
ginger

1 tsp. minced fresh garlic

¹/₂ tsp. 5-spice powder

¹/₈ c. ketchup

¹/₄ c. cold water

Place all ingredients in a food processor and blend until smooth, about 1 minute ◆ Chill until ready to serve.

GREEN PAPAYA SALAD

¹/₄ c. sushi vinegar

¹/₈ c. sugar

1 tsp. minced fresh ginger

¹/₄ tsp. salt

1 c. peeled, seeded, and finely
julienned fresh green papaya

¹/₄ c. peeled, seeded, and
finely julienned fresh mango

1 small red bell pepper,
finely julienned

1 Tbsp. chopped cilantro

¹/₄ tsp. sambal oelek
(Indonesian chile paste;
if unavailable, use chile paste)

Place vinegar, sugar, ginger, and salt in a medium mixing bowl and whisk until the sugar has dissolved, about 1 minute ◆ Add remaining ingredients and toss ◆ Cover and chill at least 2 hours before serving.

4 4-oz. skinless, boneless fresh
opah fillets

1 c. Asian Barbecue Sauce

Marinate *opah* steaks in half of sauce in a small shallow bowl ◆ Cover and refrigerate for 2 to 4 hours ◆ Preheat grill ◆ Remove steaks from marinade and discard marinade ◆ Grill each side of opah steaks for 3 to 4 minutes, or until golden brown.

Place a small bowl with remaining barbecue sauce in center of a large platter ◆ Arrange Green Papaya–Maui Mango Salad around bowl, and arrange steaks around salad ◆ Garnish platter with fried julienned won ton skins, black sesame seeds, and fresh sunflower sprouts.

Serves 2.

Sautéed 'Ōpakapaka with Spiced Rum–Maui Pineapple Butter Sauce

MAUI PINEAPPLE SALSA

3/4 c. finely diced Maui pineapple

2 Tbsp. finely diced Maui onion (or Vidalia or Wala Wala onion)

2 Tbsp. chopped fresh cilantro

1/4 c. sweet Thai chile sauce (available at Asian markets)

Combine all ingredients in a medium bowl ❧ Cover and refrigerate. (Salsa can be made a day ahead for more flavor.)

SPICED RUM–MAUI PINEAPPLE BUTTER SAUCE

1 c. chopped fresh Maui pineapple

1 c. mirin (sweet Japanese rice wine)

2 Tbsp. canola oil

2 Tbsp. chopped Maui onion (or Vidalia or Wala Wala onion)

1/2 c. spiced rum (Captain Morgan brand, if available)

1/2 c. heavy whipping cream

1/4 lb. unsalted butter

1/2 tsp. salt

1/4 tsp. white pepper

Place pineapple and mirin in a blender; blend until smooth, about 45 seconds ❧ Heat canola oil in a medium saucepan over medium heat ❧ Add onions and lightly brown, about 30 seconds ❧ Add rum and increase heat to high; let alcohol burn off ❧ Add pineapple mixture to pan and bring to a boil ❧ Reduce heat and simmer for 10 minutes ❧ Add cream and simmer until thickened, about 15 minutes more ❧ Slowly whisk in butter ❧ Season with salt and pepper ❧ Remove from heat and strain through a fine sieve or cheesecloth.

1/4 c. canola oil

2 7-oz. skinless, boneless fresh 'ōpakapaka fillets

1/2 c. flour seasoned with salt and pepper

2 servings your favorite cooked starch

Heat canola oil in a sauté pan over medium heat ❧ Dredge 'ōpakapaka fillets in seasoned flour; lightly brown both sides until fillets are cooked to medium doneness, 3 to 4 minutes on each side depending on thickness of fillets ❧ Remove fillets from pan and place on paper towels to absorb excess oil.

Place starch in center of a warm dinner plate ❧ Place fillet on top and ladle half of Spiced Rum–Maui Pineapple Butter Sauce over it ❧ Serve with steamed fresh vegetables around fish ❧ Garnish with Maui Pineapple Salsa and chopped fresh curly-leaf parsley.

Serves 2

'Ōpakapaka is the pink snapper of the Pacific and the crown jewel of all fish, by far my favorite. It is a light, delicate, moist, and flaky deepwater fish. If pink snapper is unavailable, try onaga (red snapper) or uku (gray snapper).

Shutome (also known as broadbill swordfish) is great on the grill. It has a steak-like texture and is easy to cook. I created this hulihuli marinade for the Taste of Lahaina in 2004 and won first place for my Hulihuli Lamb. The marinade is excellent for summer barbecues. Huli usually refers to rotisserie cooking over an open flame and was originally done with chicken, but over the years the recipes have changed. This is my own twist on an old Hawaiian favorite.

Hulihuli Shutome

MARINADE

½ c. soy sauce

2 Tbsp. minced fresh ginger

2 Tbsp. minced fresh garlic

¼ c. red wine vinegar

1 tsp. whole black peppercorns

1 bay leaf

¼ c. orange-*liliko'i* (passion fruit) juice concentrate (or orange juice concentrate)

2 Tbsp. minced fresh lemongrass bulb (or 1 Tbsp. fresh lemon zest)

¼ c. canola oil

Place all ingredients in a blender and blend at high speed until smooth, about 1 minute.

4 6-oz. skinless, boneless fresh *shutome* steaks

Place *shutome* in a medium mixing bowl; pour marinade over the steaks ❧ Cover and refrigerate for 2 hours.

Make sure grill is very clean and preheat to medium-high ❧ Grill steaks about 2 minutes on each side, until just cooked through.

Serve with Tako-Shiitake Kim Chee (see Soups and Salads) or Cucumber-Mango Namasu (see Maui Napoléon Poke Trio Salad) ❧ *Pohā* Berry Dipping Sauce (see Crisp Purple Sweet Potato–Crusted *Lehi*) would also be a great complement ❧ Garnish with fresh microgreens and toasted sesame seeds.

Serves 4.

GLOSSARY OF HAWAIIAN FISH and best cooking methods

'Ahi

'Ahi refers to two species: big-eye tuna (*Thunnus obesus*) and yellowfin tuna (*Thunnus albacares*). I prefer yellowfin as it tends to be firmer and better for cooking.

Yellowfin Tuna

'Ahi is found from the ocean surface to depths of about 100 fathoms. Caught year round in Hawai'i's waters, yellowfin is most abundant during the summer season (May–September). Its flesh coloration varies from pink in smaller fish to deeper red in larger fish, which typically have a higher fat content. Yellowfin in Hawai'i range from 3 to over 200 pounds in weight.

Cooking: Yellowfin is best grilled or smoked. Larger fish are prized for sashimi grade.

'Ehu

(*Hachijo akamutsu*)

Also called yellow-striped red snapper, 'ehu inhabits deep reefs from 600 to 1,000 feet throughout most of the Pacific. It can range in size but is preferred between 5 and 10 pounds. 'Ehu has always been a highly valued fish in

Hawai'i. Its bright red color means good luck in Asian culture and the fish is often served on ceremonial occasions. 'Ehu is delicate and sumptuous, yet lesser known than ōpakapaka.

Cooking: 'Ehu is great pan-fried or baked, or can be steamed or deep-fried.

Hamachi

(*Seriola spp.*)

Hamachi is also known as yellowtail. In a heated discussion with a sushi-chef friend of mine, Tommy, he tried to convince me over a few drinks that yellowtail is part of the tuna family—let's just say he drank for free the next time we met.

Hamachi weighs an average of 4 to 6 pounds. Its distinct buttery flavor and high fat content are prized among sushi chefs.

Cooking: Grilling and smoking are popular techniques, and chefs all over the world are now experimenting with new and exciting recipes for this highly versatile, delicious fish.

Hāpu'upu'u

(*Epinephelus quernus*)

Commonly called grouper or sea bass, hāpu'upu'u is a deepwater bottom fish usually found at between 50 and

150 fathoms. Most caught off the main Hawaiian islands range from 5 to 10 pounds in size, whereas the waters around the Northwestern Hawaiian islands yield fish from 10 to 30 pounds. In general, larger fish are caught at greater depths.

Hāpuʻupuʻu is noted for its clear white flesh, which is almost as delicate in taste as that of Hawaiʻi's deep-sea snappers.

Cooking: Steaming is a favorite method of preparing *hāpuʻupuʻu* in Hawaiʻi (especially smaller fish). It is also good baked, poached, or deep-fried in batter, or is sometimes served raw as ceviche.

Hebi
(Tetrapturus angustirostris)

Commonly known as short-bill spearfish, its dorsal fin is shorter than that of other billfish, and its bill is almost non-existent. Most *hebi* caught in Hawaiian waters are between 20 and 40 pounds in weight.

Its flesh is softer and more delicate than most billfish, and its flavor is mild.

Cooking: Smoking is best, followed by marinating and grilling.

Lehi
(Aphareus rutilans)

Also known as silver-mouth or iron-jaw snapper, *lehi* looks similar to *ōpakapaka* with the exception of the tuna-like mouth. Its delicious pink fillets are slightly stronger in flavor than that of its cousins the *onaga* (long-tail snapper) and the *ōpakapaka* (pink snapper). Found in deep reefs from 350 to 600 feet, *lehi* average 3 feet in length and 32 pounds in weight.

Cooking: *Lehi* can be sautéed, broiled, baked, deep-fried, or eaten raw.

Mahimahi
(Coryphaena hippurus)

Male

Female

Commonly known as dorado or dolphinfish (not to be confused with the mammal), most *mahi* are between 8 and 25 pounds, but larger fish are caught. Fillets are usually available from local fish markets, which may carry either Atlantic or Pacific *mahi*. As long as it is fresh, you cannot go wrong.

Mahimahi is thin skinned with firm, light pink flesh. It has a delicate flavor that is almost sweet.

Cooking: *Mahi* can be grilled, sautéed, steamed, baked—you name it. This is one of the most versatile and easiest to cook of all the Hawaiian fish!

Moi
(Polydactylus sexfilis)

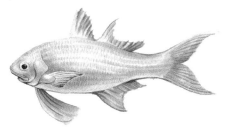

Also known as Pacific threadfin, *moi* has been farmed in Hawai'i's fishponds since the early days. In ancient Hawaiian culture, moi was reserved for the ruling chiefs and not to be consumed by the general public. Its average weight is only 1 to 1¹/₂ pounds. *Moi* has a moist, delicate flavor.

Cooking: Pan-frying or steaming is best.

Nairagi
(Tetrapturus audax)

Also known as striped marlin, most *nairagi* caught in Hawaiian waters are between 40 and 100 pounds; rarely have they been caught over 130 pounds. The flesh color of nairagi varies from fish to fish—some fillets are reddish orange while others have a lighter pink flesh.

Cooking: Reddish orange fillets are used by sushi chefs; lighter pink fillets are best grilled or smoked.

Onaga
(Etelis coruscans)

Better known by its Japanese name than by its Hawaiian name, 'ula'ula, onaga is also called ruby snapper or long-tail snapper. This bottom fish is found in deep waters. Most caught off the Hawaiian islands range from 1 to 18 pounds.

Onaga is delicate, flaky, and moist.

Cooking: Sautéing or pan-frying is best.

Ono
(Acanthocybium solandri)

Commonly known as wahoo, *ono* is a close relative of the king mackerel. It can grow to more than 100 pounds in weight, but the usual size caught in Hawai'i is between 10 and 30 pounds.

'Ono is a Hawaiian word meaning "good to eat." The fish's flesh is whiter, flakier, and more delicate in texture than the meat of other fast-swimming species.

Cooking: Grilling works best, or searing in a hot sauté pan.

Cook carefully, over high heat, until just medium rare and still translucent in the center. It is best eaten underdone, as it will dry out quickly if overcooked.

Opah
(Lampris regius)

Also known as moonfish, *opah* is one of the most colorful of the commercial species available in Hawai'i. A silvery gray upper shades to a rose red dotted with white spots toward the belly. Its fins are crimson, and its large eyes are encircled with gold. The moonfish's large, round profile may be the origin of its name. Moonfish in Hawai'i range from 60 to over 200 pounds in weight. Its fillets are moist, pink, and delicious.

Cooking: The freshest *opah* is used for sashimi, broiling, and occasionally smoking.

Ōpakapaka
(Pristipomoides filamentosus)

Though commonly known as crimson snapper or Hawaiian pink snapper, the skin of *ōpakapaka* is light brown. This species occurs throughout the tropical Pacific, but nowhere does it grow as large as in Hawai'i. When a new *ōpaka-paka* fishing area is discovered, the initial size of fish caught may be 12 to 18 pounds—*ōpakapaka* of this size could be at least 10 years old.

Like onaga, *ōpakapaka* is delicate, flaky, and moist.

Cooking: Sautéing or pan-frying is best.

Pāpio
(Chaetodon ornatissimus)

Also known as baby *ulua*, pompano, or juvenile jack (when under 10 pounds), *pāpio* is generally caught by rod along the shoreline. It is a favorite in the islands among both locals and visitors. *Pāpio* is a tender, flaky white fish with a mild flavor.

Cooking: *Pāpio* is best pan-fried or baked, but is also great deep-fried.

Rainbow Runner
(Elagatis bipinnulata)

Rainbow runner is also known in Hawai'i as *kamanu* or Hawaiian salmon. Often mistaken to be in the salmon family, it is actually one of 200 different species of the jack family, which are found in tropical waters worldwide. The largest recorded specimen caught in Hawaiian waters was 3½ feet in length and 23 pounds in weight. Rainbow runner has light pink, moist fillets.

Cooking: Fresh rainbow runner is prized for sashimi. It is also great for grilling or frying.

Shutome
(Xiphias gladius)

Also known as broad-bill swordfish, *shutome* is the most widely distributed of all billfish in the Pacific Ocean. It ranges from 10 to over 90 pounds in weight. *Shutome* has a tender, steak-like texture and is very mild in taste.

Cooking: Grilling or pan-searing is best.

Tilapia
(Tilapia guinasana)

Tilapia is widely distributed around the world and has a diet of mainly aquatic plants. It attains a total length of about 17 inches and weighs up to 5½ pounds. The mild flavor and medium texture of this fish have become so popular, it is now the 6th most consumed fish in the world.

Cooking: Tilapia can be baked, broiled, pan-seared, or steamed.

Uku
(Aprion virescens)

Uku is commonly known as gray snapper or jobfish. Among Hawai'i's most popular deepwater snapper species, *uku* occurs at the shallowest depths—usually less than 60 fathoms.

Most of the *uku* catch is between 4 and 18 pounds in weight. Fishermen rarely catch *uku* less than 1 to 2 pounds, or over 30 pounds. Like the other snappers, *uku* is delicate, flaky, and moist.

Cooking: Sautéing or pan-frying is best.

RESOURCES

All Star Produce
808-873-9299
315 Ho'ohana Street, Unit 1
Kahului, HI 96732

Eskimo Candy
808-879-5686
2665 Wai Wai Place
Kīhei, HI 96753

The Fish Market Maui
808-665-9895
3600 Lower Honoapi'ilani
Highway
Lahaina, HI 96761

Fresh Island Herbs
www.freshislandherbs.com
808-572-1771

Indian Harvest
www.indianharvest.com
800-294-2433
Indian Harvest
Specialtifoods, Inc.
P.O. Box 428
Bemidji, MN 56619

Island Plantations
www.islandplantations.com
retail store:
808-593-2035

Welcome to The Islands
Ward Centre
1200 Ala Moana Boulevard
Honolulu, HI 96814

Maui Chef
www.MauiChef.com
808-669-1503
181 Hui F. Road #43
Lahaina, HI 96761

**Maui Oma
Coffee Roasting**
www.hawaiicoffee.net
808-871-8664
800-900-9820
P.O. Box 637
Pu'unēnē, HI 96784

Surfing Goat Dairy
www.surfinggoatdairy.com
808-878-2870
3651 Ōma'opio Road
Kula, HI 96790